SAFE IN THE FATHER'S ARMS

Steve Fry

SPARROW

Sparrow Press
Nashville, Tennessee

Published 1994 in Nashville, Tennessee, by Sparrow Press, and distributed in Canada by Christian Marketing Canada, Ltd.

Printed in the United States of America

97 96 95 94 93   5 4 3 2 1

Library of Congress Cataloging-in-Publication Data:

Fry, Steve.
      Safe in the Father's arms : a 30-day devotional / Steve Fry
        p.   cm.
      ISBN 0-917143-34-5 : $9.95
      1. Providence and government of God—
      Meditations.   2. Devotional calendars.
      I. Title.
      BT135.F78   1994
      242' .2—dc20
                         93-44080
                         CIP

Song lyrics quoted in this book are from the following:

"Father of all Comfort," by Steven Fry © 1993 Steven Fry. All Rights Reserved. Used By Permission.

All Scripture quotations, unless noted otherwise, are from the Holy Bible, New International Version. © 1973, 1978, 1984 International Bible Society. Used by permission of Zondervan Bible Publishers.

Cover design by Sara Remke
Book design by Mike Goodson

CONTENTS

THE CROSSES OF OUR LIVES

INTRODUCTION

As any experienced soldier will tell you, the battlefield is where true character is defined. Under stress, character is either undone or forged. The retiring person becomes aggressive, while the one possessing great bravado loses courage. The cynic becomes a believer, the wallflower becomes a warlord, the fearful become daring, the loner becomes a comrade. A battle causes a person to dig deep within, discovering strengths and weaknesses that have lain dormant in the routine of normal life. The battle—the time of stress—is a defining moment.

The stress we face as Christians forges our spiritual character as well. Scripture teaches us that God is at work in us all the time, sending people and situations into our lives that challenge our old nature, carrying us beyond the limits of our own strength. He does this, not to harm us, but so that we will seek new strength—*new life*—from him.

This devotional is designed to help you face and overcome some of those defining, "refining" areas of your life. You may have referred to these difficult places in various ways:

• as *prisons of your life*—those times you feel trapped and unable to control your life...

• as *valleys*—those times when extreme disappointments sap your vitality and undermine your hope...

• as *crosses*—those times when you are summoned to act, not because it feels good but because it is

right, a time when you wage your greatest battle—
against your own human will.

When faced with these thresholds, there is only
one place we can stand—in the arms of Father
God, close to his heart. For there we can look
outward with confidence and inward with
contentment—because the past has lost its sting
and the future holds no fear. The fight in our heart
gives way to the rest in his arms: where our driven
soul learns wisdom and our restless mind finds
peace beyond understanding.

1

STUCK LIKE GLUE

*He who dwells in the shelter
of the Most High will rest in the
shadow of the Almighty.*

Psalm 91:1

My son loves electric trains. And recently, I put
together a model covered bridge for his train. I felt
rather good about myself, building a part of my
son's train set while he looked on in delight. With
enormous self-confidence, I took out what looked
like a simple glue compound to bond the plastic
pieces together. Feeling no need to read the
directions—I hadn't used glue in years, but what's
to remember about glue—I squeezed the tube and
began pressing the pieces together oblivious to the
glue on my fingers.

Within seconds, I found my fingers thoroughly
stuck to the tube. I quickly read the directions: this
wasn't Elmer's—it was liquid cement! My fingers
were bonded to that aluminum tube. I peeled
them away one by one, slowly…painfully. Layers
of skin ripped off, leaving behind permanent
imprints on the tube…reminders of my know-it-
all attitude.

There was a spiritual message in this for me.
The fact is, we are unwittingly attached to things
in this life that were never meant to give us
ultimate security, peace and happiness. The Bible is
clear on this: everything we need for our life—
true, inner life in the spirit—comes from one

source, and that is God himself. And yet we depend on things that are not the source of life at all.

Then there is pain, when we are suddenly severed from things we rely on for our strength and security.

For instance, we build our lives on our abilities, on our accomplishments, on the material things we accumulate, or on people's good opinions of us. We feel significant if we are successful in the eyes of our peers, and base our personal esteem on whether people accept us or not. All of this binds us. Our well-being is tied to unpredictable sources, because people can like us one minute and reject us the next, and our abilities can shine in one situation and pale in another.

Most of us find security in family, jobs, bank accounts, church—none of which can substitute for the one who is the only source of genuine security. We were not created to live like that— attached to earthly forces for our spiritual strength. God drew Adam from the earth, never intending Adam to return to earth. But that's exactly what happened; sin made Adam *earth-bound.* As a consequence of his disobedience, Adam was reduced to sustaining himself by the sweat of his brow. *His life became attached to this world, his security sustained by what he did.*

When we become God's children we are "born of his Spirit." From that point on, we enter a spiritual process of maturing—that is, being slowly detached from our utter dependence on the things of this world. Often this process is stormy and painful—like having your fingers ripped from a tube of glue. God allows all kinds of trials—

rejection, misunderstandings, lost relationships, financial setbacks, harsh situations and disappointments. He does this to protect us from the greater hurt of everything or everyone we rely on letting us down. Peeling ourselves away from all earthly securities is essential if we're to press deeper into the love of God, trusting him in all things.

God wants us to find shelter and rest under his shadow. He never intended for us to be tense, frustrated or struggling, perched on a ledge of stress between anxiety and anger. When he finished creating the universe, God rested, fully intending us to enjoy that rest with him.

In Psalm 91, the psalmist longs for that inner security that only God can give:

He longs to know safe direction in spite of life's complexities.

He longs for an inner satisfaction that can't be shattered by circumstance.

He longs for peace.

In looking for that rest, the psalmist found the Lord as his shelter. The words he chose are intriguing, because they suggest protection against a storm or an enemy. Notice he says "shelter," not palace or temple. And he declares that when we *do* find God as our shelter we will then know him as our rest.

Why are the storms of life necessary? Because they drive us to shelter. Why must we endure hardships and trials? Because we are earth-bound—attached to the things of this earth, drawing our security, esteem and purpose from the world around us, from people's responses to us and from what we do. And God wants to set us free.

Our hearts indeed find their strength and rest in him. His faithfulness allows the storms, for he knows that's the only way we'll run to his everlasting arms. It is there we find ourselves… clutching his grace… holding on to the hope that only he can give…until we are stuck like glue to his never-ending love.

Think of some of the tough times you've been through lately—have you viewed them as irritating interruptions, or a chance to get closer to God?

Father God, before bringing my needs to you, before making my requests known to you, I want to praise you. I will enter your gates with thanksgiving and your courts with praise. My need to praise you is not based on my emotions, but on the fact that you are worthy to receive it.

Your Word says that as the heavens are high above the earth, so your ways are higher than mine. Lead me now, Father, to understand your ways… lead me on the path of wisdom…that I may never cease to praise you.

2

RESTORING THE WONDER

Like a weaned child is my soul within me.

Psalm 131:2

Not long ago, my wife Nancy woke me early
one morning to announce that our baby was ready
to enter the world. Later that day, we looked into
the face of a bright-eyed cherub, our new little girl.
We were ready to brave the sleepless nights, ready
to endure hectic days, ready to die for this angelic
child with whom God had graced our home.

It's been awhile since we've had a newborn
around—Cameron is eight and Kelsey is six. As
she nestled in her mother's arms, I found myself
musing on the wonderful innocence of childhood,
and how easily it can be shattered as we grow up.

Sometimes I'm not so sure about this business
of being an adult. Childhood has some advantages.
Children have a built-in sense of adventure, a
willingness to risk. As we go through life, though,
we run into enough painful circumstances that we
build higher and thicker walls around our heart.
We discover that openness with others often leaves
us vulnerable to their criticism—and slowly we
close ourselves off. Before we know it, we have
sacrificed intimacy, and we find ourselves more
and more guarded, eventually alone.

In terms of our achievements and self-worth,

we set out to tackle great challenges, dream big dreams, and we expect big payoffs. But after awhile, we miss the mark enough times that our mental, emotional, even physical resources are depleted. After enough failures, facing one more challenge can reduce us to panic, or it can cause us to become bullish and domineering.

In many ways, we live with the fallout of anger or anxiety. To protect ourselves from risk, we beat a slow retreat into those safe, predictable zones. We are not as honest with others, not as trusting, not as adventurous. What has happened?

Our inability to control the way other people see us, or to control the outcome of our hard work, causes us to cut back our lives to what we can handle. Slowly, imperceptibly, we withdraw. We find that we have lost our sense of wonder. Most tragic of all, we also put limits on God.

Or maybe we never really *knew* the truth: that no matter what happens to us, God is in control, and "in all things God works for the good of those who love him…" (Rom. 8:28).

There is a way to discover a childlike ability to trust, a way to find new adventure in living. At first, the way to this new freedom may seem contradictory, for it may mean that God allows us disappointment, or seasons of feeling handicapped or trapped, or will call us to an unpleasant place of obedience, precisely because he wants to restore to us the power that comes when we trust him in childlike innocence.

Specifically, we will look at three men who endured great tests but emerged with a stronger hold on living within the sheltering presence of

God. First, we want to look at the apostle Paul in prison; for we, too, are trapped by adverse circumstances beyond our control. Second, we will look at Moses at a time when he endured great disappointment; for we also experience disappointments that drain the thrill of living. Third, we want to look closely at our Lord Jesus on the cross; for we are called to carry our own crosses so that we might discover a greater freedom than we have ever known—a resurrection life in spirit.

Rather than hoping for a miraculous change in your life, ask God to use the difficult experiences to give you satisfaction and contentment—a miracle in spirit no less than the greatest of God's works! The things that have robbed us of our peace and happiness are the things God uses to restore the childlike wonder that is life to our souls …if we let him.

Are you willing to begin with God on a new adventure in living? Are you willing to learn, like others who have led the way in faith, how to release the control of your life into God's hands?

Take a moment to recall some of your happiest childhood memories —do you believe that God is able to restore that joy to you now?

Create in me the heart of a spiritual child—a heart that can trust, a heart that can bounce back even when bruised…that sees people as potential friends not as potential enemies…that rests in the provision of its Father…that sings and laughs uninhibitedly.
There is nothing too hard for you, oh God. So give me the heart of a child, that I may really know you as my Father.

3

OUR "PRISONS"

...I am in chains for Christ.

Philippians 1:13

He has sent me to bind up the brokenhearted, to proclaim freedom for the captives and release...for the prisoners.

Isaiah 61:1

It was a dark hour for England, during the early stages of World War II, when German forces trapped thousands of British soldiers at Dunkirk. With the enemy all around them, it was either surrender or be pushed into the sea. For Britain's new prime minister, Winston Churchill, the situation looked bleak. Precisely at this point of impossibility, the pluck of the people and the courage of their leader was aroused. Churchill's evacuation of British troops at Dunkirk is one of the most memorable images from that war. It was during that brilliant, dangerous operation that Churchill delivered his famous address, some say the most powerful of his career—just thirteen words, directed to those battle-weary troops: *"Never give up...never, never give up! Never, never, never, never give up!"*

We've all experienced times when there seems to be no way out. That feeling of being trapped is frightening. Some feel trapped in an unhappy marriage or in a financial struggle, or paralyzed by memories. Others are confined by broken dreams, betrayal, failure, bad choices, lack of skills or the right "breaks" in life. We, too, may find ourselves in a struggle between the realization that we might have been wrong after all, and all we have done has been so much wasted motion… and the tiresome prospect of getting back on our feet, so emotionally spent that we can't take a step forward or backwards.

How we see all these limitations has an enormous impact on our spirit. I once asked a psychiatrist, a Stanford graduate and a committed believer, to identify the root cause of depression. He told me that after years of counseling he had concluded that the primary cause of clinical depression is a feeling of being trapped—of losing control over one's life. It comes from the feeling that nothing can heal our heartache or assuage the pain that gnaws on our nerves, eats away our will, devours our confidence and steals our hope.

Are we seeing the circumstances of our lives in a wrong light? Is it possible that even the circumstances we don't like can take on God's design if we allow them to bring us face to face with ourselves and with who God is? In tough circumstances we discover things about God and about ourselves that nothing else can teach us. A prison can be a productive place if we perceive it correctly.

I'm not talking about hard-nosed endurance, or learning an assortment of psychological coping mechanisms—grim determination, a fatalistic attitude, ambivalent withdrawal or denial of the hardship. Nor am I talking about trying to "think yourself happy" or mechanically quoting Scripture as some kind of charm that transports you beyond pain. I am talking about what God can do *in* you, as you yield to him in the midst of your circumstances.

Maybe it's time for a new strategy—a new type of spiritual courage. Will you allow God to work in your personal circumstances—to give you the kind of freedom the world can never take away? For the Christian there is a way out—and that way is to discover a deeper faith in God.

Instead of changing your circumstances, change your heart! Maybe it's time to look at harmful attitudes and values, and to keenly focus your attention on God. Let him lift your eyes above all your limitations and give you a new sensitivity to his presence—a new conviction that your life is not out of control but fully under his control.

When faced with unpleasant circumstances beyond your control, do you chafe under them or praise the Lord through them?

Oh Lord, give me eyes to see things the way you see them. So much of the time, I perceive things on a surface level and never look deeper to understand your purposes. I don't like some of the circumstances I am in. But I don't want to remain the way I am, so I am willing to change. I am willing to stop fighting my circumstances and allow you to show me what you are doing in my life. Even though I don't understand it all, I am willing to learn. As you open my eyes to see, also soften my heart to understand.

CRAWLING IN THE SLOW LANE

Your attitude should be the same as that of Christ Jesus: Who...made himself nothing, taking the very nature of a servant, being made in human likeness. And being found in appearance as a man, he humbled himself...

Philippians 2:5–8

We are enthralled by mythical heroes and superstars—perhaps because they are what we want to be. We want to live with no limitations. We don't like to face the truth that there are some things we cannot do. But when we reach the limits of our own strength, we touch the place where the limitless power of the Holy Spirit takes over.

A man of action like the apostle Paul must have been frustrated as he sat chained between two prison guards in a Roman cell. Before his arrest, he fathered young churches and mentored other leaders. He knew what it was like to see a godless city like Ephesus come to its knees, to provoke the Jewish believers to embrace God's mission to the Gentiles. Yet here he was, chained between two soldiers—unable to preach, to execute strategies, even to pore over his precious scrolls of Scripture.

Frustration like that can lead to depression. But with his spiritual perception, Paul looked deeper than the surface of circumstances because he understood the ways of God. He understood that his activities had been curtailed for a divine purpose. Because he was in God's hands, he knew his present limitation was God's plan for his life. And so we find him vigorously witnessing to the prison guards, seeing one after another come to faith in Jesus Christ.

We often struggle with our limits, especially those that seem unjust. We either get angry with God for imposing the limits or we fatalistically accept them. Yet, those limitations are really God's way of preparing us for something new. Perhaps *contentment with our limits* cultivates a creative peace that turns obstacles into opportunities. Our limitations bring us to the point of need—where we can find the fresh beginnings of *miracle.*

Engineers who plan to turn a two-lane road into a six-lane freeway must first reduce the two lanes into one so the road crew has room to work. That one-lane road is inconvenient for awhile—but the benefits of the wider freeway eventually erase the memory of that temporary limitation.

God has a broad way for each one of us —but in order to get there, he first has to restrict us to the one-lane road of trust in him. Are you willing to accept his plan, and to allow God to focus your attention on new opportunities in your life?

Accepting this challenge requires us to have our spiritual eyes opened to a truth filled with wonder: God does not dogmatically order us to walk a narrow way—instead, he walked the narrowest, hardest road first, to show us how.

God chose to limit himself to a human form, in the person of Jesus Christ. Jesus fully accepted that limitation. Here we come face to face with the *humility* of God —he limited himself for our salvation, and the humility was so deep it led Jesus to a cross. He walked this dark, painful path to bring us into friendship with himself.

Humble people are comfortable with themselves, free from concern about what others think. They accept correction easily because their self-esteem isn't tied to what others think about them. Aware of personal limitations, they know when to reach out to others for help, discovering in return how enriching interdependence can be. They wait for others to recognize their gifts, rather than trumpeting them themselves.

When we take the humble attitude of Christ in our limitations, as Paul did, we experience the power of the one who was limited for our sake. Our eyes open to the opportunity to identify with the one who took upon himself human frailty and found complete favor with God. We will know the inner delight of being like Jesus.

The spirit of humility is freedom. If only we will recognize that our limits are God's design.

When you look in the mirror and face your limitations, are they a source of dissatisfaction or an incentive to seek God's strength?

Lord, I have many limitations. And sometimes I feel trapped, handicapped. Help me sense what you want to do in my life. May I recognize you in my circumstances, and keep me from becoming angry with you and with others. Help me, like Paul, to be content in all things. Father, shine the truth of your goodness into my heart, and set my sights on your love for me—not on my circumstances.

CLOSING CHAPTERS

*But even if I am being poured out
like a drink offering on the sacrifice...
I am glad and rejoice.*

Philippians 2:17

Can you remember when your first romance ended? When your best friend moved away? When your kids left for college? Or when your company relocated you?

It's hard to see things we love come to an end —good relationships, meaningful projects, things that enrich our lives with happiness and meaning. But inevitably, certain chapters in our lives close. And it hurts.

Paul's arrest and captivity in a Roman cell marked the close of a great chapter in his life. The mission that had so consumed him—the conversion of the Gentile world—was now abruptly curtailed. Now he was no longer able to debate in the synagogues, wrestle with the intellectual issues of the day on Mars Hill or lovingly instruct new disciples in their walk with Jesus.

When a chapter of our life closes, the changes can be troubling. We feel lost, and we search for answers. This period—transition—has a peculiar darkness all its own.

But during transition, when once comfortable routines lose their satisfaction, when we are restless and bewildered—when an inner shift of spirit takes place—then we sense the greatness of our changeless God!

Paul discovered something in that Roman prison, probably early in his imprisonment. I think he learned, in a turn on that familiar maxim, that the more things change, the more *Jesus* stays the same.

We proclaim that Jesus Christ is the same yesterday, today and forever—but the power that comes from the changelessness of Christ can never fully be ours until we have gone through round after round of changes.

How was it that Paul could say to the Philippians that he prayed for them to be "filled with the fruit of righteousness that comes through Jesus Christ" (Phil. 1:11)? That phrase, *filled with the fruit of righteousness,* seems an odd choice for Paul, the prisoner. What kind of fruit could he bear? What kind of ministry could he have in that dank Roman cell? Perhaps by the time he was thrown into this dungeon, Paul understood the changelessness of God through the many changes of his life. And now he could draw on God's sovereign control over his life. Paul saw that in the midst of any change in his life Jesus Christ *was* still the same.

The Holy Spirit of Jesus, who brought the city of Ephesus to its knees, would exercise that same kind of power, though in a different way, in a Roman prison. The fruit of righteousness, Paul knew, would be just as plentiful here as it was when thousands at Lystra instantaneously responded to his ministry. He knew the truth that

Jeremiah had uttered so long ago that those who
trust in the Lord "will be like a tree planted by the
water…It has no worries in a year of drought and
never fails to bear fruit" (Jer. 17:8).

Only as we go through transitions—coming to
terms with closing a chapter and opening a new
one—do we come face to face with the
changelessness of Christ. In a world where chapters
open and close frequently, we search for stability,
certainty, assurance. Many look for a bedrock in a
world of quicksand. Those of us who have seen
that the more things change, the more Jesus stays
the same will be like a tree… yielding its fruit in
due season.

Are you finding it difficult emotionally to
manage all the many areas of your life? Do you
need to simplify things by reducing your
responsibilities and interests?

Lord, grant me wisdom to know how to close
chapters in my life. To know when to move on to new
endeavors, or when to cultivate new friends. And
how to graciously adjust to the changes. I wish things
would stay the same—but life isn't like that. Your
Word tells me that I am a pilgrim in a strange land,
and even now I am preparing for an eternal life
with you.

Help me remain rooted in you, and open to your
new work in my life. Change my circumstances
whenever you choose. And grant me the grace to yield
to those changes without being consumed by regret or
uncertainty about my future.

6

OUR ULTIMATE CONFIDENCE

*I always pray with joy…being confident of
this, that he who began a good work…will
carry it on to completion…*

Philippians 1:4, 6

Where does real confidence come from? I'm
talking about the kind of confidence that looks life
in the eye and grins no matter what. Paul possessed
resilience, hope and steadfastness, in a way that
defied the severity of his circumstance. His
confidence enabled him to say:

*I have learned to be content whatever the
circumstances (Phil. 4:11).*

My God will meet all your needs (Phil. 4:19).

*For to me, to live is Christ and to die is gain
(Phil. 1:21).*

His letter to the Philippians is full of
encouraging one-liners. Where did his confidence
come from? Either Paul had an obnoxious
optimism that flew in the face of reason, or he had
been transformed. No doubt some transformation
had occurred, because Paul was absolutely sure that
*the Lord was able to complete and perform the work
he started in him and the young church in Philippi.*
With this assurance, he rejoiced —and he prayed.
Paul was confident that God was totally in control,
even while God was out of the picture.

As part of our positive-thinking culture, we like

to think that God is in the business of helping us find ways out of problems, rather than leading us into them. Consider this: what if God designs confining, inhibiting circumstances to produce unique treasures in us? Maybe we need to go beyond the idea that God uses the prisons in our lives, and assert that God *plans* limiting circumstances just for us!

God allowed Paul his prison experience so that we could have his comforting letter to the Philippians. He took Paul away from the hectic pace of his labors, set him aside and got him to write. Paul may not have seen the full picture of what God was doing, but he knew this—God was in control.

Likewise, our confidence comes from knowing Christ will complete his work in us. It is in the prison, in those circumstances where we feel trapped and unable to do it ourselves, that we learn it is God who calls, enables, equips, motivates, energizes and coordinates. And God who releases his resources to complete the work.

When we realize that God is the author and the finisher, we will be content knowing that our present trials have meaning.

As believers, we should never doubt our future, never become hopeless about our tomorrows. We walk hand in hand with God, and even our failures cannot thwart him. Humbly bring all your failures to him—and watch him turn them into strengths. We are not called to create our future, but to know the author of our future. Cultivate a relationship with the Lord—nothing will be written about your future unless he writes it.

When was the last time you felt truly confident about your life and where it was headed? Have you been trying to build a life or are you leaning on the Master Builder, Jesus Christ?

God, you are my strength and my song, my author and finisher, the one who will complete a good work in me. I never need to face the future with uncertainty. I never should doubt what you are doing, for you are in me to will and to do of your good pleasure. Even if I feel insecure or put on-hold, I can rest in this: by your Spirit I am destined to fulfill your purpose for me.

You are a God of power, and when I feel stifled or weighed down by things that sap me of spiritual vitality, even when I have to walk through the consequences of past mistakes—you still are able to complete your work, and I will be victorious in you.

7

THE MONSTER WITHIN

Some preach Christ out of envy
and rivalry…supposing that
they can stir up trouble for me…

Philippians 1:15, 17

My grace is sufficient for you.

2 Corinthians 12:9

The oldest of three siblings, I had some obvious advantages while growing up. Particularly at times when I'd pin my younger sister down and tickle the living daylights out of her. It was fun for me, of course, but not for her. She'd kick and scream and try to squirm away, while I'd take fiendish delight in her distress. She was livid, and I loved it!

When we face circumstances we can't change, or a person we can't escape, our initial reaction is to get angry, to fight. We want to kick the cat—or anyone else nearby. Some people show their anger by nursing grudges, others become vengeful, looking for a scapegoat to blame. Some seethe within and withdraw. Some become intolerable complainers. Some blame themselves for their situation, regardless of whether or not it was their fault. Others blame God and turn away from him.

Paul's confinement became even more miserable when he heard that false apostles were visiting the churches he had established and for which he so greatly sacrificed. Apparently these false apostles were spreading lies about him, ravaging his reputation and spoiling the hearts of those he had spiritually fathered. Helplessly sitting by while his life's work was dismantled had to feel like a kick to the stomach.

When life goes against us, often monster rage within us screams, "Unfair!" Maybe if we get mad enough, we think, we'll get God's attention…

Why does the angry monster within us rage? Usually, we get angry when someone blocks our goals, crosses our will or keeps us from a reward we feel is rightly ours. Somebody beats us to the punch, or rips us off—and we boil over inside.

Inherent in our modern value system is the right to pursue personal fulfillment and happiness. But with that right comes responsibility —for now our happiness and well-being is up to us. If someone gets in our way, we must fight to protect our domain. Deep within us lies a spiritually toxic assumption—that we are the only ones who can make ourselves happy. No wonder limitations provoke a torrent of rage.

But God allows prison experiences in our lives to show us how reliant we are on our own strength.

Paul had discovered it was at the point of his weakness that Christ's power was released in him. He found God's grace in the face of hardship gives us:

- inexplicable peace
- enthusiasm to forgive
- an optimism that finds good in all things
- an adventurous attitude that looks to see how God works all things together for his loving purposes.

Anger in the face of limiting, confining circumstances merely exposes our self-reliance. And that is the real monster within, from which God wants to free us.

Do you frequently react to life's irritants with anger or frustration? Have you considered that God may be allowing stressful situations to bring those hidden roots of anger to the surface?

Lord, my anger is sometimes too powerful for me to withstand on my own. When I feel backed into a corner, or when my dreams are suddenly obliterated, it seems unjust, and it is hard not to get angry—at you, at others, but most of all, at myself.

One by one, Lord, I bring to you everything that provokes anger in me. I give you my anger, and receive your peace.

8

RELEASE

*I know that…what has happened
to me will turn out for my deliverance.*

Philippians 1:19

It was a forbidding place, this massive prison edifice that loomed before us, dirty and in disrepair. We were led through its gates, then through several security checks. I noticed the worn look on the guards' faces as they methodically went about their business. They seemed as imprisoned as the felons they guarded. Olmos Prison, a maximum security facility in La Plata, Argentina, is "home" to murderers, child molesters and rapists. Squalid and overcrowded, the cells are not a likely place for the fires of spiritual revival to burn…

It was after I walked through the final checkpoint that I heard it—a sound like I've never heard before. As I walked toward the chapel, it crescendoed to an overpowering chorus—the sound of men singing at the top of their lungs. More than singing, it was the sound of *praise*. This was unlike any church choir I'd heard. I walked through the chapel door and was met with a deafening wall of worship! Almost a thousand men stretched hands to the heavens and lifted faces to God. I began to weep. There was a Presence there that exuded pure love, and it was overwhelming!

Here were men, many of whom had been incarcerated for a long time, demonstrating a joy and a faith unknown to many of us in the stressed and busy pace of the world outside the walls.

I sat down and felt wave after wave of God's love sweep over me, bathing me in the undiluted holiness of his glory!

This was what all of us long for, search for, hope for. *I had found the sublime—in the squalor of a prison.* In this penitentiary that housed three thousand once-hard-core criminals, I found a brotherhood of some one thousand born-again believers—the largest "prison church" in the world.

What was it that I had seen in their faces when they prayed for me? It was *freedom.* Their freedom resulted from an undistracted preoccupation with the Lord. And this prison church has a mission: to duplicate what they have done in prisons around the globe. Some of the prisoners are writing books about God's freedom that will be published around the world. The young man who is their pastor is starting a similar prison church in the penitentiary at Juarez, Mexico. Their single-minded passion for God is sobering in the light of how easily distracted I am.

These prisoners offer us a valuable insight: God allows prison experiences in our lives so that he might slowly eliminate all our worldly distractions. And by taking away distractions, he brings us the freedom that comes from having a single focus.

Often, what we call *freedom* is merely the prerogative of self-absorption. We may think this is freedom, but ultimately we find ourselves incessantly analyzing our needs, solving our problems, building our esteem, until we find ourselves caught in the darkest hole of all—self-centeredness. To free us from that bondage, God orchestrates circumstances to bring us greater freedom.

Sometimes we feel confined to a dreary corner of loneliness. But when we accept that God allows us the experience, a curious thing happens: the place of isolation produces an inner sense of freedom. In the late Third Century, Anthony, one of the earliest Christian monks, felt God calling him to the desert, away from the growing worldliness of the Church of his day. During those years of isolation, he realized that much of his life was built on empty conceits and temporal values. As he focused on God, he experienced greater freedom from within. His needs became simpler, his concerns fewer. Slowly, he was released from things that rob us of peace—anxiety, competitiveness, comparison with others, worries about our future, the drive to succeed—until enjoying God was all that mattered.

Paul discovered the same thing: He was confident that what had happened to him would turn out for his salvation. To the Hebrew mind, salvation was far more than a temporal deliverance from an unwanted circumstance, or a salvation to some eternal destination only. Rather, salvation was comprehensive—it was past, present and future. Paul realized, even as he wrote, that his confinement was *saving him from himself.*

Paul must have wrestled with his imprisonment at first. But he soon saw that the physical limitation was an opportunity to soar over anxiety, disappointment, anger.

We want to soar, don't we? Yet so often our reactions to life make us feel more like animals trapped in a snare. The more we struggle, the deeper the snare digs in. When we finally realize the pain we're inflicting on ourselves, we cease struggling and wait patiently to be set loose. The moment we stop wrestling with our circumstances, we discover God's rest...and our true freedom.

In fact, our prisons can reveal to us those actions, attitudes, even personality traits that have been shaped by our
- fear of others' displeasure
- need to be affirmed
- attempts to gain the respect of others.

Nothing in the universe can separate us from the love and freedom that God offers. No wonder Paul could rejoice. No wonder he told us to rejoice! We of all people on the earth can celebrate, because even in our most severe limitation we have significance in Christ...and we know the power of a spirit that is released to soar.

Rejoicing can be difficult at times—when you feel least like doing it, that's the time you need it most.

Father, I am amazed at your wisdom. To think that you allow limitations, setbacks and handicaps, to bring me into greater freedom. But such is the profound way you work.

Changing my heart when I can't change my circumstances disciplines me to remain in peace and constantly cultivate contentment. Thank you that you don't run to change my circumstances every time I call. Thank you that you use the people and circumstances in my life to expose my heart and set me free.

9

ADVANCING

*What has happened to me has really
served to advance the gospel.*

Philippians 1:12

Lying awake at three A.M., I was gripped by a panic that mercilessly shook my insides. For months, I had watched the slow collapse of almost every source of security in my life. Relationships were unraveling, income was dropping and sleeplessness was becoming chronic.

What made this struggle so painful was that I could do nothing about it. I couldn't get out of my circumstances and I couldn't change them. I had felt trapped in this disheartening place for almost a year.

There I was, awake, caught in a maelstrom of anxiety. Beyond that stretched a terrible despair. Was all my work for nothing?

I forced myself to recall Psalm 23: "The Lord is my shepherd…" As a boy, I had often quoted the gentle words of the beloved psalm. Now, as I lay awake and shaken, a melody came to me and I began to sing, "The Lord is my shepherd." I got out of bed, made my way to the piano and began to write a simple but hauntingly beautiful melody for the words taken right from Scripture. Immediately, I felt the soothing touch of the heavenly shepherd, restoring me.

Nine months after my sleepless night of anxiety and despair, I accepted an invitation from the German Embassy in Washington, D.C., to perform my musical, "Thy Kingdom Come." They were celebrating German reunification in a series of concerts on the Embassy grounds, and had asked me to be their "religious" guest. The evening of the concert the Embassy ballroom was packed with diplomats, Embassy personnel, opera singers and others. It was a privilege to share the good news of Jesus with people there who perhaps did not know him.

When it came time to conclude the evening, I spontaneously rolled the grand piano to the center of the stage. I invited the guests to sing with me the song I had written—the Twenty-third Psalm. The peace of God seemed to touch that audience, and a hush fell over the room. In it, I could sense the sweetness of the Father's presence.

Later, I recalled the painful circumstances in which this song was written. Now I had seen the penetrating effect it had on my listeners at the Embassy. I told the Lord, "If it took that kind of hurt to produce something that touches people in this way, I would go through it again!" Even in one of the darkest nights of my life, God had been at work, bringing fruit from my life, even though I couldn't see it.

Paul knew that what happened to him was meant to advance the gospel. His joy came, in part, from his confidence that his setbacks actually furthered the cause—he had staked his life on it. Paul was not paralyzed by regret. He knew that the purposes of God could not be hindered.

It's freeing to live with purpose. No matter what you and I will ever walk through, we need never be stripped of our significance. Nothing can rob us of that. In Christ, we can't lose! Because at the point of our most intense emotional captivity, God is there to further his work in us, through us, *for* us.

The issue is always how much we let God do through us. At the end of the day, the one who seizes every failure as an opportunity for good will be the winner.

Do you see negative situations as setbacks, or as God's sovereign way of redirecting you to higher purposes?

I thank you, Lord, that you are never limited. Even when I feel stuck, you are working to advance your kingdom. I don't always know how you do that, but I am content simply knowing that you do.

Help me to see that every circumstance of life is an opportunity to be a partner with you in the advancement of your kingdom. I never have to feel insignificant. I never have to let the enemy rob me of my sense of purpose. I can always feel content… because nothing I encounter can limit you.

LOSING IT ALL
TO GAIN IT ALL

*I consider everything a loss
compared to the surpassing
greatness of knowing Christ...*

Philippians 3:8

*Servants of God...poor, yet making
many rich; having nothing, and
yet possessing everything.*

2 Corinthians 6:4, 10

Paul surveyed his life prior to his conversion
and declared it a complete loss, as compared to
knowing Christ Jesus. Always to the point, Paul
minced no words here. He expressed utter
disregard for his life without Christ—including all
of his past, with his vast accomplishments. Was he
being dramatic? Or had he discovered a key to life
that gave him an exuberance and freedom.

Paul's secret was this: By considering everything
nothing compared to knowing Christ, he
neutralized regret on one hand and false comfort
on the other.

Recently, I had to come to terms with regret
over an event that occurred a couple of years
before. I had been presented with a great
opportunity, but it came along at a time when I
was discouraged and worn out. I had been

disappointed by well-meaning friends, and felt frustrated with life in general. In the weariness of the moment, I turned down the opportunity. Only later did I see that it would have resulted in my significant long-term success. Instead, I had settled for a short-term pity break.

For some time, I had buried the regret, but through a series of probing encounters with the Lord I had to squarely face my disappointment. It wasn't easy, and I found myself agonizing over what might have been had I made a different choice. There is nothing so paralyzing as the *what-might-have-beens*. But as I reflected on Philippians 3, I suddenly comprehended the truth that so captivated Paul: that everything in the past can be—*must be*—jettisoned for the present pursuit of the Lord Jesus himself. Had I not made the choice I did, but instead made the one that led to greater success, I would still be asked to consider *that* a loss, as much as the disappointment.

God directs me to consider my disappointments inconsequential compared to knowing Jesus. It's only natural that we will feel regret for those things that might have been. But what might have been doesn't matter any longer! That's freedom.

A little later on, Paul gave a classic summary of his life: "Forgetting what is behind...I press on toward the goal..." (Phil. 3: 13-14).

Paul knew that the past can stifle us. And he said that we can lay hold of the life for which Christ has laid hold of us—which is to know him in the power of his resurrection.

When we become nervous that we are slipping behind our peers, or when we feel the itch to carve our niche, we judge ourselves by a false standard. These things need not pollute our spirit.

If we are to know Jesus in a way that cultivates hope and releases faith, we must consider everything a loss. Then we can neutralize our disappointments and know freedom from regret.

Take a hard look at your past...every success, every disappointment; every good choice and bad choice. For a moment, imagine yourself tying them all up into a great big bundle and throwing them into the ocean of God's grace. Now turn your back on them and walk into the arms of Jesus, empty-handed but free.

How deserving of praise you are, Lord! Your children, of all people, have cause to rejoice—for our past never has to have power over us. I praise you for the greatness of your redeeming love. And right now I bring to you all my failures and my successes. In view of your greatness, I toss these things over my shoulder and come to you empty-handed.

Fill me with the joy of knowing you, and with eager anticipation for my future, which you are even now designing. I want to press on to the prize. No matter what has gone on before, I am not disqualified in the race...therefore, I take hold of your promises anew. Confidently, I look towards a future of walking hand in hand with you, doing whatever you ask me to do.

11

A CHANGE OF PERSPECTIVE

Their mind is on earthly things.
But our citizenship is in heaven.

Philippians 3:19-20

I was sixteen, and had crossed a significant
threshold of adolescence—I had my driver's
license! Sitting behind the wheel of my '65 Chevy
Impala, pedal to the metal, radio blaring, I was the
envy of my friends.

At that time, my home church, where my
father pastored, sponsored a Bible conference with
an internationally renowned teacher. I was in awe
of this woman. Her teaching challenged me and
brought about a major change in my life. During
the conference, she and her husband invited me to
join them for lunch. I was to follow them to the
restaurant—in my '65 Chevy. Driving along, I
was minding everything *but* my driving when
suddenly they turned into a parking lot. By the
time I saw their brake lights it was too late. I
slammed on my brakes— to no avail. I plowed
into that automobile—the one owned by that
renowned Bible teacher! I was petrified.

I'll never forget my humiliation as I looked up
and saw her slowly bow her head. I wasn't sure
whether she was praying, collecting her wits or
counting to ten. My hunch was that she was asking

God for grace to respond kindly to my stupidity. And that's precisely what she did.

Experiencing her patient response affected me even more than her teaching. I saw her faith worked out in life. She saw this unfortunate event as an opportunity to show godly patience to a bumbling sixteen year old. She *responded to God* instead of *reacting to the circumstance.*

Many times I have been a reactor... sometimes the nuclear kind! I have viewed adverse circumstances as pesky interruptions in my agenda. I have viewed failures as setbacks to my success, seen a belligerent neighbor as an adversary, viewed my government's tactics as political manipulation.

But there are spiritual realities behind these things, and we grow strong as we learn to see life from a spiritual perspective. What is genuine spirituality? What does it mean to be "spiritual?" We usually think of it as doing what is right. We consider a spiritual person good, right and morally correct. Yet spirituality not only has to do with being moral, but also and more fundamentally, with having a correct understanding of life. It has to do with a change of perspective, seeing our lives from a wholly different frame of reference.

Paul had a heavenly perspective. He knew where his citizenship was registered. He understood that he was seated with Christ in heavenly places, and so he exhorts us: "Do not conform any longer to the pattern of this world, but be transformed by the renewing of your mind" (Rom. 12:2). Don't be conformed to the value system of this world, don't see things only from a human, fleshly point of view. See things from *God's* point of view.

Paul saw life through those different lenses. His perspective had been radically altered, and he realized that though he was bound by circumstances, he was free to commune with God, free to pray for others in distant lands, free to love his enemies.

The spiritually mature don't react to life as events happen to them. They don't see life as a series of random events over which they have little control. When difficulties press in, the spiritually mature understand what is behind the difficulties. Conflict, whether from a testy landlord or an obnoxious co-worker, is seen for what it is—a struggle not against flesh and blood but against principalities and powers of darkness. Resisting the enemy's provocation, the spiritually mature ask God to strengthen their hearts.

We expend so much energy trying to be spiritually mature, trying to live right, when the first step is to allow the Holy Spirit to change our thinking. If we *thought* maturely, it would be easier to *act* maturely. As long as we perceive life only from this earthly plane, as long as we react to life instead of respond to God, we will forever be trying to be spiritually mature without inner spiritual power.

We need to stop and say, "God help me to be renewed in my mind, help me to see things from a heavenly perspective. Help me to be so heavenly minded that I *will* be some earthly good."

Do you see people and events in your life as they appear to be initially, or do you try to understand the spiritual realities behind them?

Father, forgive me for not always seeing things from your perspective. Forgive me for not taking the time in prayer, or in meditation on your Word, to cultivate a spiritual view. Forgive me for not seeing the one who becomes irritable with me as someone with spiritual needs; for seeing unbelievers as adversaries and not lost men and women; for becoming angry with government officials or impatient with racial unrest. I forget that we do not wrestle against flesh and blood, but against principalities and powers in spiritual places.

I need to cultivate a spiritual view of things— therefore, I will spend more time with you, so that I may see things the way you see them.

Ruling From Prison

*I can do everything through
him who gives me strength.*

Philippians 4:13

Like a runaway train racing pell-mell along a
gritty track, our emotions sometimes take us on a
wild ride through life. One moment we're
chugging uphill, feeling weary and despondent;
the next, we're careering down the other side in
elation—or panic!

One of life's great challenges is learning how to
control our emotions. But, as most of us have
discovered, that is not always easy. For some of us,
our feelings have been our god, ruling us through
fear, anger or fleshly pleasures.

We believers have to make a decision: Who is
going to rule us—Jesus or our emotions? That is
one of the most important questions we'll ever
answer.

So you are feeling down. You wish you had a
different personality or a better looking face.
Maybe you're facing an unexpected pregnancy and
don't know how you're going to feed another child.
Or you never had a chance to finish college. It is
time to ask, *Who is Lord—Jesus or your emotions?
Who is greater—God or your anxiety, anger,
disappointment or regret?*

Limitations are a gift from God because they
give us a chance to bring our emotions under the

control of the Holy Spirit. Are you ready to make this statement:

As a true believer in the Lord Jesus, I must confess that God is greater than my fear, greater than my resentment. Therefore, I will praise him, and I will rejoice. If I cannot do that, then it is an admission that God isn't as great as my anger, my fear or my regret. God is either greater or he is not—and I must now make that decision.

Paul told the Philippians he had learned to be content in all circumstances. He had recognized that God is greater than any other power. Were his circumstances going to control him? Were people's opinions going to control him? Were his emotions going to control him? No, because Jesus was his Lord!

How do you respond when you feel backed in a corner? Is your dominant emotion anger? Resentment? Apathy? Overwhelming melancholy? Or maybe you simply ignore things and look the other way.

We must have a healthy ruthlessness with ourselves. We cannot afford to negotiate or compromise with our emotions—we have to stare them down, with the continuous affirmation that Christ is Lord.

Who or what really rules you? Your anger, your anxiety, your envy—or the Lord Jesus?

Lord, I confess my tendency to give in to my emotions. In this moment, I accept your challenge: I believe you, Lord Jesus, are more powerful than my anger, anxiety, envy, sadness or depression. While I cannot deny the reality of my emotions, I refuse to let them dominate me.

It doesn't matter whether the emotions remain or not—what matters is that you are Lord. I know that in time my emotions will come under your control and I will know joy and peace. Not only that, but I will receive wisdom to address the issues that provoke negative emotions. And in this way I can truly overcome.

13

DISAPPOINTMENT'S DESTINATION

When the Lord finished speaking to Moses on Mount Sinai, he gave him…the tablets of stone inscribed by the finger of God…Then the Lord said to Moses, "Go down, because your people, whom you brought up out of Egypt, have become corrupt."

Exodus 31:18, 32:7

If you were offered heart-to-heart friendship with God, wouldn't you go for it?

Moses had a passion to know God. He knew that his innermost longings would only be satisfied in an abiding friendship with the Lord. Nowhere was that longing more eloquently expressed than when Moses, alone on Mount Sinai, cried out, "O Lord, show me your glory!"

What brought Moses to this place of spiritual hunger? What was it that launched him on his journey to "the glory of God?" To discover that we must go back a bit.

For forty days, Moses had been alone with God, excitedly watching as God laid out a blueprint by which a whole nation could enjoy divine blessing. These were not the dry dictations of a distant God who wanted his creatures to obey his every whim, or the passionless mandates of a judge communicating laws. Here was a loving Father,

designing a spiritual environment in which his
children could thrive and be happy.

And during this tender time, the Israelites were
far away at the foot of Sinai, building their golden
calf. We are stunned by people who had seen God's
hand of deliverance and were afraid of his presence
on Sinai—yet so quickly forgot all this, pooled
their golden earrings to make an idol and declared
that idol responsible for bringing them out of
Egypt.

The shock to the heart of God must be
something like what parents feel when a child
rebels with obstinate fury, or what we feel when
betrayed by a trusted friend to whom we've
confided our most intimate feelings.
Brokenhearted, God said to Moses, "Go down
because your people, whom you brought out of
Egypt, have become corrupt."

At that moment Moses, too, must have felt the
sting of disappointment. Moses had anticipated
Pharaoh's attack, had prepared himself for the
rigors of leading the people across a barren desert,
had steeled himself against the opposition of the
devil. But this was so unexpected—this outright
rejection of the God who had so graciously
displayed his power on their behalf!

Sometimes we are stunned by unexpected
disappointments. Disappointment can come like a
thief in the night, puncturing our expectations
when they are at their highest. This can be
devastating. Moses must have felt a sickening blow
to the gut when he saw God's people creating an
idol for themselves. And yet this unexpected
disappointment led Moses to the crest of divine
encounter.

As we follow Moses on his journey from this staggering disappointment to his glimpse of God's glory, ask God to show you how unexpected disappointments call you to a deeper, more intimate relationship with him.

Have you had any disappointments that you've been unwilling to face? If so, take time to let the Lord show you the new things he wants to do in your life.

Lord, show me how past disappointments have affected me. Have I unknowingly buried things, causing me to react to people in unhealthy ways? Or have I unconsciously developed negative attitudes because of some hurt I have never come to terms with? Have I allowed my heart to grow hard? Have I lowered my expectations, so as not to get hurt again? Or have I withdrawn from anyone simply because they disappointed me? If so, reveal it to me, as I wait on you.

Responding out of a wounded spirit can damage others and destroy me. Show me where I need to receive your healing—and be whole again.

14

FREEDOM FROM OURSELVES

"I have seen these people," the Lord said to Moses, "and they are a stiff-necked people. Now leave me alone...that I may destroy them. Then I will make you into a great nation."

Exodus 32:9-10

One of today's most widely-read authors had this to say about the way people deal with pain:

> When real life presents us with painful experiences...when something hurts us...when we feel unfulfilled—we feel cheated. And too many of us—too often —reach for instant happiness by illegitimate means that disregard the interests of other people. (Scott Peck, author of *The Road Less Traveled*)

It's true. One of our first reactions to disappointment is to secure our own happiness at any cost, even if it means focusing on ourselves at the expense of other people.

God offered Moses instant gratification when he vowed to annihilate the source of Moses's disappointment—the rebellious people. And if that were not enough, God promised to make Moses great—to birth a whole new nation through him that would eventually provide redemption for the entire planet. Incredible!

Was God playing games with Moses—merely testing his humility? No, God meant business. On the line was his plan to redeem the planet. God needed people who would bear his name no matter what. With this proposal, God said to Moses, "I see in you what I need to further my purposes." He asked Moses to consider his potential, his gifts, his personal destiny. In light of severe disappointment, who among us wouldn't take comfort in a vote of confidence from the Creator himself?

When we are hurt, we react by closing ourselves off from any further exposure to hurt. We refocus our attention on the one thing that we can be sure of—ourselves. When we are disappointed with someone, rather than focus on rebuilding that relationship, we often look to our own interests. It is easy in the face of hurt to take Polonius's advice in Shakespeare's masterpiece, *Hamlet*. "To thine own self be true."

Moses could have done that. Instead, his response was pristine in its innocence. He asked, "Why should the Egyptians say, 'It was with evil intent that he brought them out, to kill them in the mountains and to wipe them off the face of the earth'"(Ex. 32:12). Moses meant, *God, what will the nations say if you do this thing?* Moses was more concerned with God's reputation than with his own opportunity. He was preoccupied with making sure God was glorified, rather than his reaching his personal potential.

If we focus on ourselves and nurture our own potential, we must accept responsibility for the outcome...even if we fall flat on our face. If we keep our focus on the Lord, however, we can rest in his control over our lives. This is a necessary step on our way to the dwelling place of the most high…the place of abandonment, where even our personal potential takes a back seat to God's glory.

Have you taken that step? Have you surveyed all your potential, your goals and dreams, then gathered them up and handed them all to God? Are you willing to give up what seems best for you, to seek instead the glory and honor of God?

Take time today to examine your heart—how much time do you spend thinking about yourself, your desires, your needs or working out your own problems? And then consider: how much time do you spend thinking of others and meditating on God's goodness?

Sometimes, Lord, I think only of myself. It's easy for me to withdraw into my own world at times. I don't want to get involved in people's lives much anymore because of the risk.

Forgive me when I'm self-centered or preoccupied with my own agenda. Grant me the courage to risk again. Fill me with your love for others, so I can once again be involved in their lives, even comforting them in times of disappointment. For I know that the most fulfilled life is the life given away.

15

THE THRESHOLD
OF BITTERNESS

*When Moses approached the camp
and saw the calf...his anger burned
and he threw the tablets out of his
hands, breaking them to pieces
at the foot of the mountain.*

Exodus 32:19

Moses' return to the camp brought
overwhelming disappointment with God's people.
In a rage, he threw the tablets of stone on the
ground. Understandable, we say. He had a *right* to
be angry.

Yet those tablets represented the covenant word
of God. In a moment of anger, Moses allowed
bitterness to dominate—and he smashed the
tablets. No doubt Moses was right to confront the
rebellion of the people. But in doing so he
discarded something God gave him in sacred trust.

I know a woman who has every right to be
bitter at the way she has been treated, even by
Christians. Yet her faith teaches me extraordinary
lessons.

Only in her late thirties, Susan's life reads like a
screenplay. Abused as a young girl by both her
father and grandfather, she nonetheless excelled
academically. Graduating early, she found herself
facing university life at the tender age of fifteen.
There she pursued all kinds of religions, even
exploring the occult. One night as she walked

through the campus, a van full of young men pulled up beside her, abducted her and raped her.

A few days after the attack, she came upon some students passing out tracts and telling people about Jesus. As she confessed her deep hurts and needs, they prayed with her and she found Christ.

When she returned the next day, she found others preaching on the street corner. Wanting to know more about the Lord, she joined them, unaware that they weren't from the same group as the students who led her to Christ, but instead were from one of the more toxic cults, the Children of God.

Susan's trek with the cult took her overseas, where she found herself virtually a slave to the group. Miraculously, she escaped to the west coast of Africa, where she began using her musical talents, giving evangelistic concerts and ministering in prisons and hospitals. She eventually married one of the musicians—a professing believer—who worked alongside her in ministry.

Her marriage soured after her husband ordered their unborn child, their third, aborted while she was in the hospital undergoing treatment for an illness. Later, Susan learned that he had another wife and children—who were pressuring him to get rid of Susan.

Finally, with her two young children, she made her way back to eastern Canada, where she found Jesus again. There, she married a good man, and began a solid ministry among the people of the inner city of Toronto.

If anyone had a right to be bitter, Susan did. But there is no sign of bitterness in her today as she leads people to Jesus in Toronto.

Few of us go through such torment as Susan—but at times we all have felt we had a right to be bitter. Perhaps it is hardest to resist bitterness when we're wounded by the selfish actions or rude remarks of a fellow believer. Christians shouldn't treat us this way!

Disappointment, when it leads to bitterness, can cause us to destroy the sacred things in our lives. We soon turn from the promises of God to denounce the people of God. It's easy to say to God, "You don't care about me, and your promises really don't mean anything." Once that happens, you may find yourself discarding the promises God has given you and forfeiting that place of faith you have been cultivating. Then, although you may pass the threshold of bitterness, you may have to chisel out God's promises again, just as Moses had to chisel out the tablets a second time. Trying to rise to God's promises a second time is sometimes more painstaking and requires more effort.

Watch that your disappointments not lead you on the path of bitterness—away from God's people, or from God's promises.

Is there any area in your life where you have allowed yourself to become bitter? Is there any individual or group of people that seems to be a constant source of resentment?

Lord, sometimes I battle bitterness. Open my eyes to what you want to do in and through me in this time of disappointment. Cleanse me of the infection caused by holding grudges. Grant me faith to forgive and discard all resentments.

16

FORSAKING IT ALL

Moses went back to the Lord and said, "Oh, what a great sin these people have committed!...But now, please forgive their sin—but if not, then blot me out of the book you have written."

Exodus 32:31–32

For Moses, the path to God's glory first led to depths few ever reach. Once he recovered from his anger that led him to break the tablets, he announced to the people, "I will go up to the Lord; perhaps I can make atonement for your sin" (Ex. 32:30).

What transpired next between Moses and God takes us terrifyingly close to the smoking chasm of self-sacrifice...

where love is shaped by humility's demands,
where faith is summoned by suffering,
where a King becomes a baby,
a cross becomes a throne,
and hell is invaded for a heavenly
purpose.

Moses offered God an all-or-nothing proposition. Because he knew the consequence of an eternity without God, a debate must have raged within him: *Should I go through with this?* Face to face with God again, he cried out, "Forgive my people... but if not, then remove my name from the book of life." Amazing!

Who can imagine the amazing sacrifices God calls out of us when we truly love someone? When Moses climbed back up the mountain, he knew full well that God required a lamb for an atoning sacrifice. Yet he went empty-handed, willing to be the sacrifice for his people, the substitute for their sin and rebellion.

In other words, *he was willing to bear the consequences of the people's sin and rebellion himself.* One by one, Moses laid down his dreams and God's promises, much as Abraham had done with his son Isaac. All he had hoped for, all he had envisioned—he laid it all down.

How does this speak to us? How do we bear the consequences of others' faults, mistakes and sins? By patiently enduring their criticism, allowing them to vent their anger, while remaining kind and open-hearted, so that they will be emotionally released to find Jesus. By becoming the scapegoat, the one on whom blame is laid, we can bring about reconciliation.

It's unlikely we will be called on to exchange our eternal salvation for the sake of someone we love. But the pathway to God's glory leads to this: sacrificing our dreams, ourselves if necessary, for the sake of others. If we want to see God's glory, we may be led to the precipice of self-sacrificing love.

Instead of working to resolve our disappointments, God may ask us to graciously endure them—and to present ourselves to him, to receive his transforming, forgiving love.

Are you presently faced with the challenge of loving someone despite the way they've treated

*you? Or is there anyone in your life to whom you
need to express unconditional acceptance, and
whose faults and weaknesses you need to overlook?*

*What a privilege—this invitation to be like you,
Jesus. Living as you lived may at times require that I
bear the consequences of others' sins and mistakes.
Thank you in advance for patience in the face of
provocation, for grace when confronted with
grumbling, for loyalty when others are fickle. When
disappointment comes, walk closely with me, and let
your redeeming power flow through me.*

17

WANDERING WITH GOD

*Then the Lord said to Moses,
"Leave this place, you and the
people...and go up to the land..."*

Exodus 33:1

Life is so unstable. It must have seemed so for
Moses and the million vagabonds he led. After
their thrilling exodus from Egypt, they still were
unsettled, homeless, in transition. Moses already
had spent forty years wandering in the desert
tending sheep before he was sent by God back to
his Egyptian homeland—and here he was again,
unsettled, in transition.

Times of transition can be tough. We draw our
sense of security from the familiar and the routine.
We are easily coddled in the lap of predictability.
But suddenly the wind of God whips up, seizing
our sails and driving us into uncharted waters.

Oddly, even when our circumstances are
uncomfortable, we are even less comfortable with
change. False comfort is hypnotic—we are lulled
into a stupor, letting the inner fire of our passion
for God slowly die. Our sense of purpose wanes,
our future becomes fuzzy and faith goes cold.

Change disrupts our sense of security. We feel
shaken, stunned, alone. Suddenly, we are without
familiar landmarks, feeling adrift. Cut loose in this
way, we sense that we have lost our moorings, our
anchor, our *hope*.

But when life turns upside down, God wants to draw close to us as a friend. In times of wandering, we can cultivate friendship with God. How did Moses become God's friend? By wandering in the wilderness. How did Paul become God's friend? By "wandering" in Tarsus for years until Barnabus remembered him and told the other apostles about him. Each one must have felt alone, lacking in direction. But they knew that they must pursue God, and did not waver in their commitment to his purposes.

Memories from my past can fence me in—and fence God out—keeping me from growing in understanding. I build "temples" to preserve my last encounter with God, so I can bask in that moment for a lifetime.

But God moves us onward. We are pilgrims in a strange land, and if we become too much at ease with our surroundings, the roses whose fragrance we've enjoyed begin to fade, the brook whose waters refreshed us dries up, our garden becomes a desert. Then we are forced to walk under the heat of the sun, pressing on to the next oasis where God meets us again. We are pilgrims, unattached to the safe land, the familiar. We see change not as threat to our well-being, but as a call to walk with God.

Isn't that the essence of faith—a willingness to wander with God?

Are you unsure of which direction to take? Has that become a source of anxiety? Will you take the time right now to re-commit your future to the Lord?

Lord, forgive me for those times I have settled for second best—when I chose security over obedience. I want so much to settle down, to sink my roots in here. But you call me to live as a pilgrim. Remind me that change is part of the adventure of walking with you, and not something to resist. I lay my job, my friends, my surroundings on the altar of obedience. I delight to walk with you.

18

IF YOUR PRESENCE IS NOT WITH US

Then Moses said to [the Lord], "If your Presence does not go with us, do not send us up from here."

Exodus 33:15

Words can't describe the exhilaration of being met at the airport after a lengthy trip by two excited children, anxious to see their daddy. It's enough to make a dad feel like a sultan. To my six-year-old daughter, that comparison is more fact than fancy—you'd think I came bearing royal gifts.

"Did you bring me a present?" she asked me as I recently returned from a trip. She was glad to have me home, but she was more interested in what I was going to give her.

Aren't we often more interested in what God does for us, than in who he is? When the pressure's on, we want *solutions* more than a sense of his presence. We want answers *from* God, rather than glimpses *of* God.

Moses' journey to the revelation of God's glory brought a more subtle challenge. God began to bless Moses and the people. He told Moses he would send his angel with them, drive out their enemies, bring them into a land flowing with milk and honey and grant them prosperity. Any of us would be amazed at such a commitment from

God. No doubt, Moses breathed a sigh of relief—
God would make good his promises. But Moses
knew this was not enough.

"If your *presence* does not go with us," Moses
responded, "then we will not go."

Many of us are satisfied with only God's
promises. As long as God comes through, we're
content. After the folly of the golden calf, surely
the Israelites were relieved to know God still would
lead them into a great homeland and drive out
their enemies.

Moses knew, however, that without God's
presence, his blessings would lull them into
spiritual passivity that would ultimately be their
undoing. Nothing is so potentially destructive as
blessing apart from the presence of God. Only a
hunger for his presence can sustain us beyond
blessing. Apart from his presence, blessing can
blind us to our deeper need and ultimately corrode
our hearts.

In a world of traffic jams, twenty-four-hour
news and Madison-Avenue hype, how do we
remain sensitive to the presence of God? Where
can we find that quiet place of the heart where we
can be refreshed in God's presence? How do we rid
ourselves of fretfulness and enter his peace? *By
spending time daily worshiping him.*

Instead of turning on the radio every time you
get in the car, try singing to the Lord. When you
feel the pressure getting to you on the job, take a
short walk and fill your mind with a favorite
worship chorus. Always remind yourself of whose
child you are. Cultivate the attitude of
thankfulness. God responds readily to a grateful
heart.

God reveals his presence to those who praise him. Thanksgiving and praise are vital first steps to cultivating sensitivity to God's presence. If we begin there, God graciously whets our appetite for him.

Are you growing in your desire to be alone with God? Does the idea of drawing close to him appeal to you? Or does it make you feel apprehensive?

Thank you, Lord, that you promised never to leave or forsake me. But sometimes I can't feel your presence. Teach me to be sensitive to you. Show me the little things I can weed out of my daily schedule to make room for private moments with you. Teach me to patiently reflect on Scripture. Help me sing songs of praise to you, and turn daily irritations into opportunities of prayer.

19

WANTING GOD FOR GOD'S SAKE

Then Moses said, "Now show me your glory."

Exodus 33:18

The first time it happened, I panicked! As a little boy, I was fed a steady diet of the imminent return of Jesus to gather up Christians to be with him. And then one day I peeked into the kitchen where just seconds before my mother had been standing—and realized she was *gone*. I called her name—no response. I ran madly through the house—no mom. When I ran out into the yard, I was screaming for my mother, but she was nowhere to be found. I thought the rapture had come and I had been left behind!

I wanted my mother's presence then, to assure me that the rapture hadn't taken place, and that I still had a chance to make it. Although, Mom was fairly incidental—*it was my security that concerned me.*

Moses, on the other hand, yearned for the closeness of God. That must have deeply satisfied God to know Moses desired, more than anything else, his presence. Listen to the joy in God's voice as he responds, "I will do the very thing you ask— my presence will go with you—because I know you by name."

And now Moses, in a spontaneous rush of desire, cries out to see God's glory. Hadn't he seen God's majestic power? Didn't he witness firsthand the deliverance of his people from one of the mightiest political powers on earth? Didn't he watch the sea part, and witness Mount Sinai erupt with trumpet blasts, lightning bolts and clouds of smoke as God's presence fell there? Hadn't he talked with God himself? What was Moses asking?

I believe Moses wanted not only God's presence, but an intimate knowledge of God himself. Moses was saying, "God I want to know what makes you *you*. I want to know what is in your heart." God must have been delighted—for opportunities to be as open as he was with Moses that day were rare. So he hid Moses in the crack of a large boulder and he revealed himself to him. What a marvel that must have been for Moses. No wonder he came down the mountain a second time with not only the law in his hands, but with the brilliance of God in his face! He had seen the glory of the Lord—and he would never be the same.

On his journey to the face of divine glory, Moses first endured unexpected disappointment. But he pressed beyond his limits, his bitterness, his needs, beyond God's promises and even God's presence, until he glimpsed the heart of God.

That glimpse evokes awe. Moses expresses a passion for God that supercedes all other desires. Beyond the discouragement of the moment, the anxiety over the future, the zeal for personal destiny, Moses simply wants to know God. He finds himself by forgetting himself. That is true freedom: to be fulfilled in the place of self-forgetting.

God does not ask us to pretend that our personal pain is a mere illusion. Instead, he leads us to a place of contentment where, when faced with bitter circumstance, deep heartbreak or even glorious destiny, *he is enough.*

Are you willing to endure great disappointment if it means cultivating a deeper friendship with God?

Precious Lord, take me to the place where I truly want you for your sake! At times I have wanted your presence so that I may be more effective in my work. I have applied spiritual disciplines for selfish reasons—to seek your blessings so I might feel more secure. Cleanse me of these motivations. Help me seek you for your sake, and delight in you simply because I love you.

20

A Place Where We Can Stand

Then the Lord said, "There is a place near me where you may stand…"

Exodus 33:21

God shelters us in a place of rest and contentment—his very heart. Because Moses expressed his longing for God's heart, God embraced him and said, "There is a place by me where you can stand."

Beyond our potential and our dreams, beyond the expectations of other people and our need for their approval is the only place of satisfaction—a place by God where we can stand.

In an increasingly uncertain world, all of us look for that place to stand. And although we wish we were John Wayne riding tall in the saddle, or Katherine Hepburn boldly staring life in the face —in reality we wilt under the blistering heat of life's disappointments.

We look for a solid place to stand, while life shifts and quakes beneath our feet. We try to stand in our own strength—putting on a brave face, running from pleasure to pleasure—but sooner or later we collapse under the weight of our own pretense. Making ourselves happy is not something we can sustain for any length of time. Eventually, we look at ourselves and realize that what we are trying to *be* and who we really *are* stand miles apart. Ultimately we have to abandon all attempts to stand in our own strength and ultimately find that place by God where we can stand.

That place is the cleft of the rock, where we are covered by his hand. To know God, and to know that our lives count, we must seek for a glory that is not found amidst the accolades of the crowd, but in a private place with God.

That may mean serving others without thanks or giving our all to some endeavor, without recognition. In the cleft in the rock, seen only by God, we find spiritual glory.

Are you willing to stand here—alone before God, serving him alone, worshiping him alone? When we seek him with all our hearts, we find that he is solid ground beneath our feet, a mighty fortress surrounding us at all times.

Have you found that place of contentment where your greatest source of comfort, enjoyment and satisfaction is the time you spend with God?

Lord, you are my rock! David proclaimed you as the one who lifted him from the miry, slippery clay and set his feet on a rock. Similarly, I know that I cannot stand in my own strength, by my own initiative, sustained even by the deepest of my desires or the greatest of my dreams. I can only stand in you.

All praise and glory is yours, God, for being that rock—not only the one on whom I stand, but the one in whom I am hid. Hide me away in you, Father—and let me see your glory...let me know your heart.

21

THE CALL TO
THE CROSS

*Let us fix our eyes on Jesus...who for the
joy set before him endured the cross…*

Hebrews 12:2

*"If anyone would come after me,
he must deny himself and take up his
cross daily and follow me."*

Luke 9:23

Obedience is one of those words that sticks to
the roof of your mouth, and refuses to go down
easy. It conjures up images of a grade-school
teacher shaking her finger in your face, insisting
you do what you're told. It backs you into a corner
and makes you sit on a stool, nose to the wall. And
it reminds you all too often of where you have
fallen short.

How can we excuse our inner resistance when
we know that obeying God is basic Christianity?

When our hearts first turn towards God, we
delight to do his bidding. It seems that most of
what he asks of us coincides with our desires. We
follow our hearts, believing the Lord is guiding us.

Then one day we come to a crossroad—we are
asked to do something for which we have
absolutely no desire. We may pray, "God, if this is
your direction, give me a sense of joy in it."

There comes a profound silence.

"Give me your peace," we ask.

Nothing.

Surely our lack of desire to do this thing indicates the inner directive is bogus. So, we ignore it. But it won't go away. We wrestle with it again and again. We feel no joy, no peace. It is at this point that we come face to face with the toughest part of our spiritual journey—the journey to the cross.

Christ's ministry was marked by the joy of communion with his Father. Obedience to his Father's will always echoed with an inner joy until Gethsemane.

There in dark Gethsemane, Jesus felt anything but joyous. Suddenly, after years of teaching, healing, delivering, saving, the cross loomed before him. His flesh and his humanity recoiled. "Father, if it is possible, let this cup pass from me," he prayed. "Nevertheless not my will but yours be done."

When we obey God's hard commands, we catch a glimpse of the cross.

We can read of Jesus' passion and crucifixion, but we cannot understand it until God's will has crossed our own. Jesus had to press through his own resistance to a cross that was utterly undesirable. Undesirable—yet still the Father's will. That is the dilemma, isn't it?

For much of my life I believed that doing God's will—though difficult at times—would bring an inner joy that more than compensated for my pain. But inevitably I come to Gethsemane, where God asks me to go far beyond myself—and there is no joy to be seen anywhere. There, lying at my feet, is a rough-looking cross. Will I pick it up and go?

Maybe you are hearing the Father's voice say to you: "I am calling you…to drink a cup, to shoulder a cross, to obey." You look, and the path ahead is not the place you want to go. You can see no immediate satisfaction, you sense no joy. But you know God is calling you.

I take comfort in the fact that Jesus struggled in Gethsemane—that he cried out three times for relief. And I call upon God, to give me tenacious faith—faith to believe him in the face of impossibility, faith that knows that beyond every cross there is life, power and hope. That hope is resurrection life in God.

Once we say, "Nevertheless, not my will but yours be done," we taste victory.

Is there an area of your life where it has been difficult to obey something you know God has told you to do?

I wish I could say that I always leap to obey your call. But the reality is that I'm afraid sometimes you'll ask me to do things or go places for which I have no desire.

Yet I know that you are my Father. Where I am unwilling, help me to be willing. Let me see beyond the challenge to obey—to the wonder of your love and the privilege of your call. Help me to learn that obeying you is my soul's greatest pleasure.

22

THE CALL TO BE LOVED BY GOD

Jesus said to his disciples, "If anyone would come after me, he must deny himself and take up his cross and follow me."

Matthew 16:24

Surrendering your will. That phrase calls up images of a life of sacrifice and a denial of all things enjoyable, doesn't it? Some of us hear the call to pick up our cross—and wince. We think bearing our cross means putting up with somebody we don't like, enduring a situation under which we chafe, or refusing some innocent pleasure we enjoy. To others, bearing a cross means punishing ourselves by rehearsing our sins, thinking that if we make ourselves miserable it will alleviate our guilt.

Surrender, sacrifice and self-denial are all part of the true *cross walk*, and sooner or later we must come to terms with them. But outward responses can become dead works, unless they are anchored in the most fundamental truth about the cross: that it is the ultimate expression of God's love.

Because of his love for you and me, God sent his Son to die on the cross. And because of his love for us, Jesus offered himself as our sacrifice. Jesus was obedient even to dying on that cross. When he went to the cross, he said, that "the world [may] learn that I love the Father" (John 14:31). As

painful as it was, everything about the cross said
LOVE.

Therefore, when Jesus calls us to take up our
cross, he first calls us to be loved by the Father. We
love him in return with an abandoned devotion
and a singular passion. When God is in the center
of our field of vision, the issue is not so much
denying self, but embracing Christ. When he calls
us to deny ourselves he asks not that we hate
ourselves, but that we change our focus. We deny
ourselves by embracing Christ —he becomes our
focus, and we find ourselves emptied of self-
centeredness.

Do you think Christ's call to deny ourselves is
the ruthless, uncaring demand of a taskmaster? If
so, think again. In fact, he calls us to be free of
preoccupation with our needs, our hang-ups, our
agenda, for he knows self-denial gives us freedom
from

anxiety over whether people like us,

fearfulness over meeting others' expectations,

anger at rejection or injustice we've
suffered,

worry about our future,

hopelessness about our past.

Trusting in his higher purposes, we no longer
feel the pressure to make something of ourselves.
Free from our concern about our own significance,
we discover with Paul, "how wide and long and
high and deep is the love of Christ" (Eph. 3:18).

"Father of All Comfort," a song I wrote while
going through one of those "stretching"
experiences expresses the joy of losing ourselves in
God's love:

Father of all comfort, come—
reveal your love.
Enfold us once again within your
everlasting arms.
Father of all comfort, we would
run to know that place
Where we are lost...if that means
being lost in you!

The call to carry our cross is a call to be loved by the Father—and to love him in return with all our heart, soul, mind and strength.

When God summons you to do something for which you have no desire, do you see that as an intrusion of God's authority or an opportunity to experience his love?

God, you are amazing! Everything you do is because of love. Even when I resist obeying you, you are there loving me. I draw close to you today. I know that everything you will allow today is for my good. By faith, I confess you to be the God who is love...and the God who loves me.

23

THE MOST DIFFICULT ACT OF FORGIVENESS

"Father, forgive them, for they do not know not what they are doing."

Luke 23:34

A frail, elderly woman walked out on stage on a warm autumn night in Jerusalem—frail, but with a marked determination to her step. Her name was Anna Grace, and I was in the audience as she told the story of how her great-grandfather, H. G. Spafford, wrote the beloved hymn, "It Is Well with My Soul."

I sat enthralled as she told us the tragic story: While on an ocean voyage, Spafford's four daughters were swept to their deaths by a storm at sea. In his grief, Spafford crossed the ocean, asking the ship's captain to stop at the spot where his daughters had drowned. It was there he penned these timeless words:

> *When peace like a river attendeth my way,*
> *When sorrows like sea billows roll—*
> *Whatever my lot, thou hast taught me to say,*
> *"It is well—it is well with my soul."*
> *(H. G. Spafford, "It Is Well with My Soul")*

Brokenhearted but not defeated, Spafford and his wife ultimately made their way to Jerusalem where they founded a children's clinic that continues to this day to care for thousands of children. But back home in America, unfounded rumors about the Spaffords's work began to circulate. Even among their own friends, their reputation was tarnished.

Hearing news of this in Jerusalem, Spafford and his wife returned home to find their own church refusing to extend them any kindness. These fellow believers went so far as to link the tragic loss of their daughters with God's judgment on their ministry.

This was a devastating blow, but the Spaffords returned to Jerusalem to continue their work with the children. In time, God marvelously vindicated them.

As Anna Grace recounted her great-grandparents' story, I thought how painful it must have been to be ostracized by friends who felt they were were justified in doing so. No doubt, forgiving those friends was difficult for the Spaffords. To forgive a vengeful enemy is tough enough—to forgive an embittered comrade is tougher still. But to forgive those who reject you and feel morally justified in their actions—that is a tough challenge!

"Father forgive them, for they do not know what they are doing," is the supreme statement of God's love, confronting the cruelty of the cross with forgiveness. And when Jesus cried "Father, forgive them...", he asked forgiveness for those who felt they were upholding the law, *who truly felt they were right in killing him.*

It is one thing to forgive those who realize they have done wrong—or to forgive those who are so clearly in the wrong that we feel vindicated even if they don't repent. But those who hurt us and feel they are right, or those who hurt us and never know they did—forgiving *those* people is hard! Our sense of justice goes unsatisfied, the ledger remains unbalanced. Forgiveness is never easy. Any time we are hurt, misunderstood or unjustly accused, it's painful. But if we want to travel on the *cross walk*, we must forgive:

• the father who criticized us to toughen us emotionally;

• the employer who is unduly harsh;

• the parishioner who creates a faction against the pastor;

• the friend who dissociates from us, merely on the basis of rumor.

Forgiveness, here, is a steep climb.

Is there anyone in your life who seems to be a constant source of hurt —someone you have difficulty forgiving?

Help me keep my eyes on the fact that you have forgiven me. For when I see how much I've been forgiven, it's easier to forgive those who have hurt me. But sometimes, Lord, the wounds go deep. And no matter how hard I try, forgiving those who have hurt me that deeply is not easy.

In those times, help me remember that you are my Father and that you understand. Even when it's hard for me to forgive, you stick with me until I get it right. Thank you that you call me to seek you all the more—until my love for you and my desire to please you is greater than my need to hold on to any unforgiveness. For when I know I'm loved by you, there is no one, no matter how they have hurt me, that I cannot forgive.

24

THE CUP OF SORROW

"Take this cup from me."

Mark 14:36

One scene in the smash musical "Les Miserables" is set in a pub in eighteenth-century Paris. There, the comrades sing a tender ballad while pledging their allegiance to each other. Exchanging glasses, they draw strength from each other, fortifying themselves for the battle they will face the next day. That moment in the musical reveals a rarity—people opening themselves in spiritual intimacy that at once unites them and fills them with courage.

There was another time when comrades shared a cup...and their master called it the cup of the New Covenant. Jesus summoned his friends to drink from a cup that represented *his shed blood*. To drink was to welcome intimacy with the giver of that cup—an intimacy that at once would unite them and fill them with courage.

And in the garden, the one who had offered his followers a cup is himself offered one. But the cup he is given in that lonely spot is not easy to drink from. This cup will mean pain and sorrow unimaginable. It is a cup of woe, hardship, rejection, isolation, betrayal. This was the cup that the Father held out to his dear Son. For this time also required a high level of intimacy, uniting Father and Son, imbuing Jesus with courage.

Isaiah called Jesus "a man of sorrows, and familiar with suffering" (53:3). For Jesus knew that the world in which he lived was not the world his Father designed. Life's delights were always tempered by the sadness of a race lost in sin. He was attuned to the harsh world of Roman occupation, sensitive to the traumas of sickness, bigotry, death.

Even when Jesus tried to reveal God's plan for people, he was rejected. Maybe that moved him to sorrow more than anything else—that with all their suffering, people still preferred darkness to light.

We spend so much time trying to manage stress, resolve sorrows and minimize hassles that we don't have much time for the Lord. If we give in to the sorrow, we find ourselves so steeped in our miseries that we lose heart for him.

It wasn't supposed to be this way.

Remember that in every melancholy moment, each sad circumstance, and turn it into a conversation with your heavenly Father. He knows what it is like to be a lover of light in a world of darkness—and he longs to be near to us at those moments when our spirit is heavy.

The hardships you endure are not simply God's means of hammering on your character—they are much more precious than that. They are to call you to intimacy with himself.

Do you find yourself constantly trying to alleviate stress? Or are you annoyed that some people keep you at a distance or even make fun of you because of your faith? Can you, now, begin to see these things as opportunities to draw close to the Lord in a new way?

What a wonderful God you are! When I encounter sorrow, you are near to me. Thank you that prayer allows me an open door to your presence even in my most difficult moments. I will see my difficulties more and more as opportunities to draw close to you. I never have to feel that you are disinterested, because your Word says you are close to the downhearted.

How privileged I am to be your child! Thank you for being my source of joy always.

25

The Cup Of Separation

*"My God, my God, why
have you forsaken me?"*

Matthew 27:46

There are times, though rare, when the call to
the cross means walking alone. It means being
misunderstood by those closest to you, and finding
no solace in the comfort of friends. The Lord
sometimes asks us to do something others
misunderstand or reject—and we find ourselves
alone, separated from those we love most.

Hudson Taylor was one of the spiritual giants of
the Church, a pioneering missionary to the Far
East, who founded the China Inland Mission. But
he was not always so respected. In the early part of
his career, he stumbled upon an idea that was to
revolutionize missionary strategy. He felt, at the
time, that missionaries were not reaching the
Chinese. He despaired at seeing Western
missionaries land in China and set up European
colonies the local people neither understood nor
cared for. From these compounds, missionaries
made sporadic forays into the surrounding
communities, trying to convert people to Christ.
But there was no serious attempt made to
understand the Chinese culture.

Hudson Taylor felt that to have an impact on
the people around him, he had to adopt their
ways, their dress—even grow his hair long enough

for pigtails, which were then fashionable for Chinese men. It was innovative, and Hudson determined to follow it through. Still,5 he was scorned by his fellow missionaries, and when he went back to England he was ridiculed. Still he knew he must identify with the culture of the people he was trying to reach.

Time has proved him right. Later in his life, many saw the wisdom of his actions. But at first, his bold step left him ostracized and rejected. It was here that young Hudson encountered that part of the *cross walk* that required standing alone for the sake of Christ.

The cross sometimes requires separation from a loved one—or at least a willingness to be separated. For Abraham it meant a lonely mountaintop where he had to demonstrate his willingness to sacrifice Isaac. For Moses it meant separation from his world and kin to go to the back side of a wilderness. For David, it meant separation as a fugitive in the desert. For Mary, it meant separation from loved ones who harbored suspicions of her infidelity. But in that place of separation each of these people found true attachment to God.

When Jesus was confronted in Gethsemane with the cup of death, the most unsavory aspect to him was that, by taking on the sins of humanity, he would risk separation from his Father. Accepting the cross meant separation from the one he loved most.

Most of us experience rejection, misunderstanding and loneliness. We may consider these the crosses we bear—but perhaps they are simply tests necessary for our maturing. However, when *in obedience to the Lord,* we find ourselves utterly alone—then we taste the cross. Walking the *cross walk,* we will at times walk alone. But when we emerge from that solitary place, we will be closer to the Father than we ever thought possible.

Have you truly, in your heart, surrendered to the Lord those you love most?

Lord, you are all that I need. You are my joy in the morning, my strength throughout the day, my comfort at night. Since you know me better than anyone else, you know what I need and when I need it. Therefore, no one satisfies me like you. I praise you for that!

Jesus, when you were on this earth there were many times you felt alone...even to the point of being separated from your Father. When I feel alone, you know what I'm going through, and are there with me. All I need to do is quiet my heart and reflect on who you are. Thank you, Lord—for the comfort that I am never alone.

26

BEING A RECONCILER

*God, who reconciled us to
himself through Christ...gave us
the ministry of reconciliation.*

2 Corinthians 5:18

Important as it may seem, I doubt if many of us
would want the job of a high-level diplomat.
Observing recent peace negotiations between Israel
and the Palestine Liberation Organization, I was
reminded of how difficult it is to reconcile
adversaries. Those negotiating the peace between
these two groups must have been stretched to the
limits of their patience. Having to listen to both
sides, trying to interpret each one's position to the
other, looking for common ground, searching for
compromises that don't sacrifice the dignity of
either party, finding the right language that
communicates to both sides, and sometimes
becoming the target of everybody's frustrations—
the process of making peace is tough.

We tend to relegate peacemaking to diplomats
or psychologists. But don't we regularly encounter
people who have strained relationships, and who
need a listening ear and a helping hand at
reconciling those relationships?

It isn't easy being a reconciler—

- getting estranged friends to bury the hatchet;
- convincing antagonistic co-workers to work
  together;

- building bridges between parents and
    children;
- healing splits between husbands and wives;
- understanding someone who comes from a
    different ethnic and cultural background;
- reconciling churches;
- finding points of contact between the
    Church and a sometimes hostile society.

Most of us don't undertake the painstaking
process of reconciliation because it depletes our
emotions and taxes our energies. That is a dear
price to pay—especially when we are not
guaranteed success. But when tempted to stay
uninvolved when faced with conflict, we hear the
call once again: "Take up your cross and follow
me."

The cross was Jesus' ultimate act of
reconciliation. We were estranged from God, the
Scriptures say, without hope of ever knowing him.
But God got involved. He made every effort to
make peace with a world of rebels—and it cost
him the life of his Son. Now, peace has been made.

Taking up the cross means becoming a
reconciler. Paul considered this his primary
ministry, a ministry given to him by God. When
Jesus said, "Blessed are the peacemakers, for they
will be called sons of God" (Matt. 5:9), he
indicated that God's children will make the
ministry of peacemaking a priority, and when they
do, they will find happiness that surpasses all
temporal delights.

It isn't always pleasant, this ministry of
reconciliation. It can require sacrifice. Sometimes
we will be the target of another's anger.

Occasionally, we may have to neglect our own interests to give attention to another's conflict. As the object of someone else's animosity, we may be tempted to pull away or sweep things under a rug. But always remember the call of the cross—to actively be about the business of reconciling people.

Do you shrink from opportunities to build bridges between people? Or are you cultivating a desire to be a peacemaker?

May I not be so concerned with my needs and my goals that I neglect to mend hurting relationships. Help me to not only nurture my own relationships, but to actively build goodwill and understanding between others. Whether I find myself withdrawing from a friend, or feel a strained relationship with a family member, or encounter others who are at odds in their relationships, grant me patience to listen, willingness to let them express anger without retaliating, insight to understand the other's views and perseverance to see the relationship restored.

27

THE SPIRIT OF
THE LAMB

*He was led like a lamb to the slaughter,
and as a sheep before her shearers is
silent, so he did not open his mouth.*

Isaiah 53:7

*Then I saw a Lamb looking as if
it had been slain, standing in
the center of the throne...*

Revelation 5:6

Facing Pilate and the cruelty of crucifixion, we find not the Lion of Judah, but the Lamb who did not open his mouth. When the apostle John saw the throne in heaven, who was the one worthy to break the seals and open the scroll? The Lamb that had been slain. As all in heaven worshiped, they fell down before the *Lamb.* As they sang the song of Moses, it was *the song of the Lamb!*

Heaven's Lion is a Lamb.

Our world doesn't place a high premium on lambs—except to shear them or eat them. Our world cheers lions. We admire those who possess power. We have an appetite for power. Whether we desire to command the masses or simply to control our circumstances or other people, that appetite can be detected by our words. Proverbs tells us that where there is much talk, sin is not far away. That warning is aimed at those of us who try to control our surroundings by what we say and how we say it.

In our journey on the *cross walk*, we need meekness strong enough to stand its ground in the face of evil, and winsome enough to be wanted by the most wounded. Pilate's attempt to manipulate Jesus with his probing questions is a classic showdown between power and humility. Jesus opened not his mouth, until he affirmed who he was to his Father's glory. Who was in control here—the Roman authority or the accused who forced this proud man to wrestle with justice and see his own hypocrisy? Jesus did not defend himself or attempt to control the outcome of the proceedings. Yet in his quiet yieldedness, it was the Lamb who roared the loudest.

When adversity comes, do you fight it, or do you yield to the Spirit? Do you try to persuade others of your opinion? Do you jump to your own defense, try to escape through cynical jesting, or find yourself stewing inside as you try to solve your problems by analyzing them to death?

By our many words, and by our wrangling, we attempt to control our dilemmas. The issue is not to control our situation, but to be controlled by the Holy Spirit. Solomon wrote, "Better a patient man than…one who takes a city" (Prov. 16:32). Here, God succinctly sets out his system of values: the greatest person is not the one with the most power, but the one who has learned to control his or her own emotions and desires.

The one who is under God's influence will be characterized by a Lamb-like spirit that has ceased trying to control the world and instead has controlled the heart. To live under Christ as Lord is to walk with Christ as Lamb, and thus become the lions who will inherit the earth.

Is humility one of your most treasured characteristics? Are you actively praying for God to increasingly develop this trait in your life?

Lord, forgive me for not trusting you enough to let my life go. In many ways, I find myself holding on to my pride—at times becoming defensive when I am corrected, unable to quickly apologize when I know I've offended someone, putting on a facade to gain another's respect and withdrawing into the cocoon of my own interests, hedging myself against unwelcome intruders. Forgive me when I am unteachable, competitive or contentious. Keep me sweet-spirited and open to others, as I let you fight my battles.

28

THE ULTIMATE QUESTION

"I have brought you glory on earth..."
John 17:4

How do we find the center of gravity in our spiritual lives? It comes down to this: Who do we live for? Whose will do we do?

Taking up the cross means submission to the Lord's will at the most difficult points in our life. The cross has little to do with daily inconveniences like preparing a tax return, or putting on a brave face in traffic or being polite to a rude neighbor. It has little to do with coping with life's complexity. Instead, we take up the cross when we obey God even when that course incurs the greatest hurt.

In Philippians 2, Paul gave us a glimpse of the attitude that bears the cross, when he called the cross Christ's ultimate response of obedience — ultimate, because it meant the greatest sacrifice.

As we wrestle daily with submission to God, the question we must ask ourselves is this: What will give God the most glory?

Choices constantly confront us. Some are easy, some are difficult. When faced with life choices— What school do I go to? What career to pursue? — or other choices forced on us by unpleasant circumstances—Do I confront the one who hurt me? Do I remain quiet about my talents, allowing

God to promote me in his time?—how do we make them? Do we say, "This choice will provide greater financial stability so that I can serve God more effectively." Or "This will make me happiest —and God said he would give me the desires of my heart."

When facing tough choices, we must ask: What would give God the most glory? If you ask that question, God will part the skies and send you an answer. In fact, he often delays answers in order to *bring* us to where we can joyfully say, "God I will go in the direction that glorifies you most." It may not be what seems to benefit us. It may not be the obvious pathway of delight. But, it will be the pathway of peace.

Some of us never quiet our hearts long enough to discern what God is doing. Then, God may let us settle at the level of spiritual maturity we choose, even if that means frolicking in a spiritual sandbox for the rest of our lives. May we instead be those who press into a relationship with God, where our desire is this: *whatever glorifies him most.*

Have you made the quest to glorify the Lord in all you do the most important objective of your life?

God, it is a privilege for me to glorify you—to exalt you in my life. When others see me, I want them to see you. I freely lay down my dreams, my goals, my desires—whatever it takes to empty me of self-interest. May I become so fascinated with you that I don't even think about myself and my needs. I commit myself to glorify you in all my decisions.

29

EYES TO SEE

We live by faith, not by sight.

2 Corinthians 5:7

Recently, my family and I made our regular pilgrimage to Disneyland. As a tot of six months, I attended the Magic Kingdom on opening day, so I feel it my duty to make an annual trek to the land of fantasy. This time, we had parked and my son—who is eight and loves Disneyland as much as I do—was barreling full-tilt towards a tram that carried visitors to the entrance.

The tram pulled away before he reached it, though, leaving him standing dejectedly. "There's not going to be another tram," he moaned as I ran up beside him.

"Of course there is, Cameron—just wait," I said.

"No, there's not! There isn't going to be another tram." he said hopelessly.

I saw an opportunity to teach him about faith. "Cameron," I said, looking intently at him, "Even though you don't *see* another tram coming—I want you to say, 'There's another tram coming.'" My rousing summons to a new frame of mind was met with melancholy silence.

"C'mon, Cameron," I coaxed. "Say it. I want to hear you say, 'There's another tram coming.'"

More silence. Finally, he looked up at me with doleful eyes and said, "But I don't see it."

Moments later, a tram did come. If Cameron had trusted me he could have saved himself some misery.

Isn't that how we react all too often? God tells us to trust him in the face of disappointment, to remember his promises in times of deprivation, to believe the goodness of his character though we see nothing but a hopeless future.

He tells us, *The tram is coming.*

We fretfully say, *I don't see it.*

Sometimes what we call doubt is, in fact, stubborn unbelief. Doubt is impressionable apprehension—it is reluctance on tip-toe, looking for assurance. Unbelief, on the other hand, is a stubborn fear—a refusal to walk on water even when the glory of Christ is in full view.

Doubt says, *God, is that you?* Unbelief says, *God I've heard, but I don't believe because my circumstances haven't changed.* Once he has given us the green light to apply a specific promise to a specific situation—and we still say, "I don't see it," that is unbelief.

As loving Father, the Lord longs to rescue us when we suffer. But often he doesn't, because that would only prolong our addiction to the temporal, material world. God wants us to learn faith. Faith is to the spiritual world what sight is to the material world. Faith is the way we see in the spirit world. Faith allows us to believe his Word, rather than the circumstances swirling around us.

We are prone to be dull to the Lord's presence, blind to his ways. In his Father-heart of love, God wants to awaken us to the Spirit's leading, even if it means leading us into darkness that we might spiritually see.

Can you look back and find times in your life when you responded in unbelief, or found it difficult to trust God's Word in the midst of difficult circumstances? Can you take a moment to thank the Lord for the ways he works faith in us during seasons of hardship, even suffering?

Lord, my own spiritual blindness makes me insensitive to my need for spiritual sight. Therefore, I depend on you to show me where I am not seeing things the way you see them.

Help me to see through the darker times of my life to what you are designing. You are the God who makes all things new, and even painful circumstances can be new beginnings. This is exactly where faith is built—in times of testing. Help me to see the problems of my life as a training ground for a lifetime of fruitful love and service to you.

30

THE GOD WHO WANTS US NEAR

*"He shall give you another
comforter...the Holy Spirit."*
John 14:16, 26 (KJV)

Before Jesus sat those who knew him best, the ones to whom he had revealed his most intimate self. These were his friends, and he knew they were about to experience grief beyond description.

In that upper room, just hours before his death, Jesus drew his friends close, to console them. At this tender moment, Jesus introduced them to the Holy Spirit. He could have used many terms to describe the Holy Spirit— "Empowerer," or "Sanctifier," or "Enabler"—but he called the Holy Spirit *Comforter*.

The term, *Comforter*, may have limited impact on us today. To us, comfort means warm jacuzzis and down pillows, an absence of pain or acquiring extras that make life "cushier." But the word *comfort* as Jesus used it has a much more profound meaning: It means *to be brought near*. It is a picture of a child cuddled in her mother's arms; a burden lifted from a laborer's shoulders; tears wiped away by a tender hand; safety in the protection of an advocate; relief that comes when God reassures you it's going to be all right.

When Paul speaks of God as the "Father...of all

comfort" (2 Cor. 1:3) he means that God wants *us near*. The Holy Spirit is called *Comforter*, because more than anything else, God wants us near to himself.

To know *his comfort*, we sometimes must first experience *discomfort*. He will try other ways to bring us near to himself, but if he can't bring us near any other way, then he allows hard things to come.

Testings and hardships are God's way of *embracing us*, not just *molding us*. It is God's method of unshackling our hearts from a world that leaves us isolated, insecure and broken.

Our greatest need is not to be empowered, or sanctified, or simply protected—our greatest need is to be brought near. When we are near to God, we will have everything.

Can you, right now, recommit every facet of your life to the Lord and begin to see that tough times are occasions to be drawn to an intimate communion with him?

Lord, I am amazed by your ways. As I reflect on the difficult seasons in my life, I remember the many times your strength was there for me, your grace held me and your love was my only sure refuge.

Looking back, I can see you are building in me an unconquerable faith, an undaunted spirit and an unquenchable desire to know you. Thank you, Father, that you've given me a place by you where I can stand!